Wildlife, Wildflowers and Wild Lands,
Wyoming Inspired, Vol.1

An adult coloring book by Belinda Daugherty
Copyright 2017, all rights reserved

For Elaine
Who always believed in my art.

Other color books by Belinda A Daugherty

Fantastic Faces, Fairie's and Frogs

WILDLIFE, WILDFLOWERS AND WILD LANDS,
WYOMING INSPIERD, VOL. 1
BY BELINDA A DAUGHERTY
TABLE OF CONTENTS

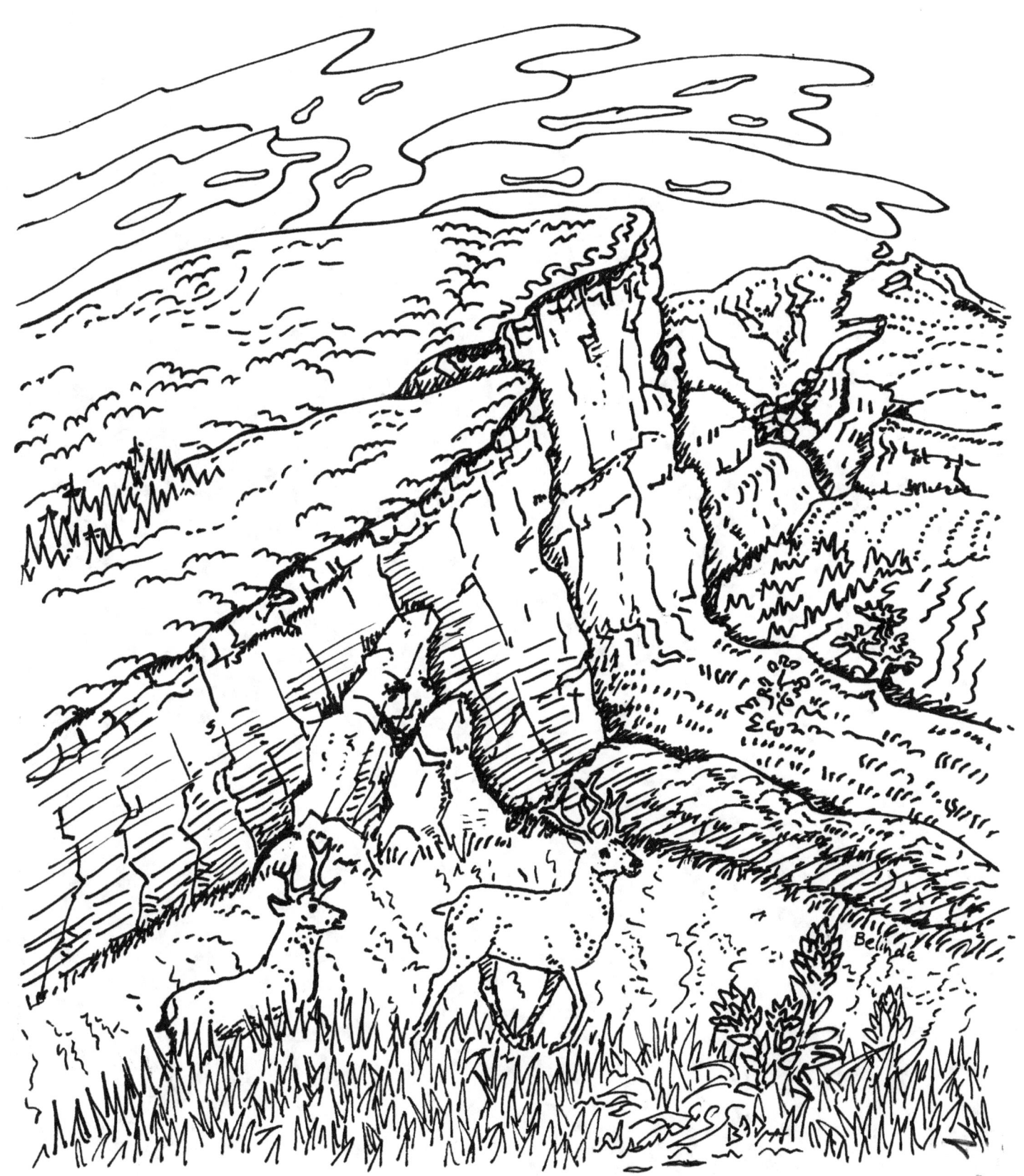

1

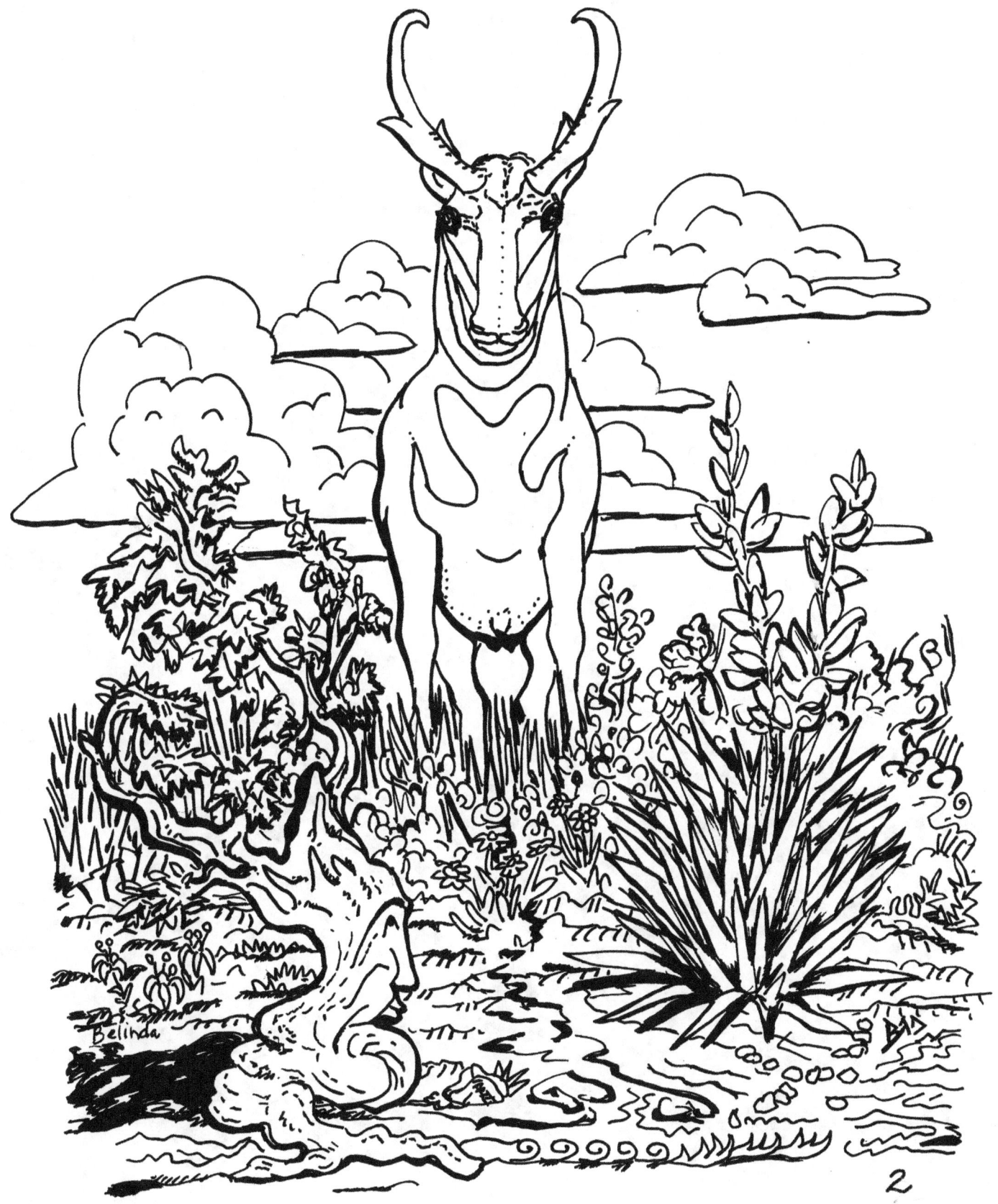

2

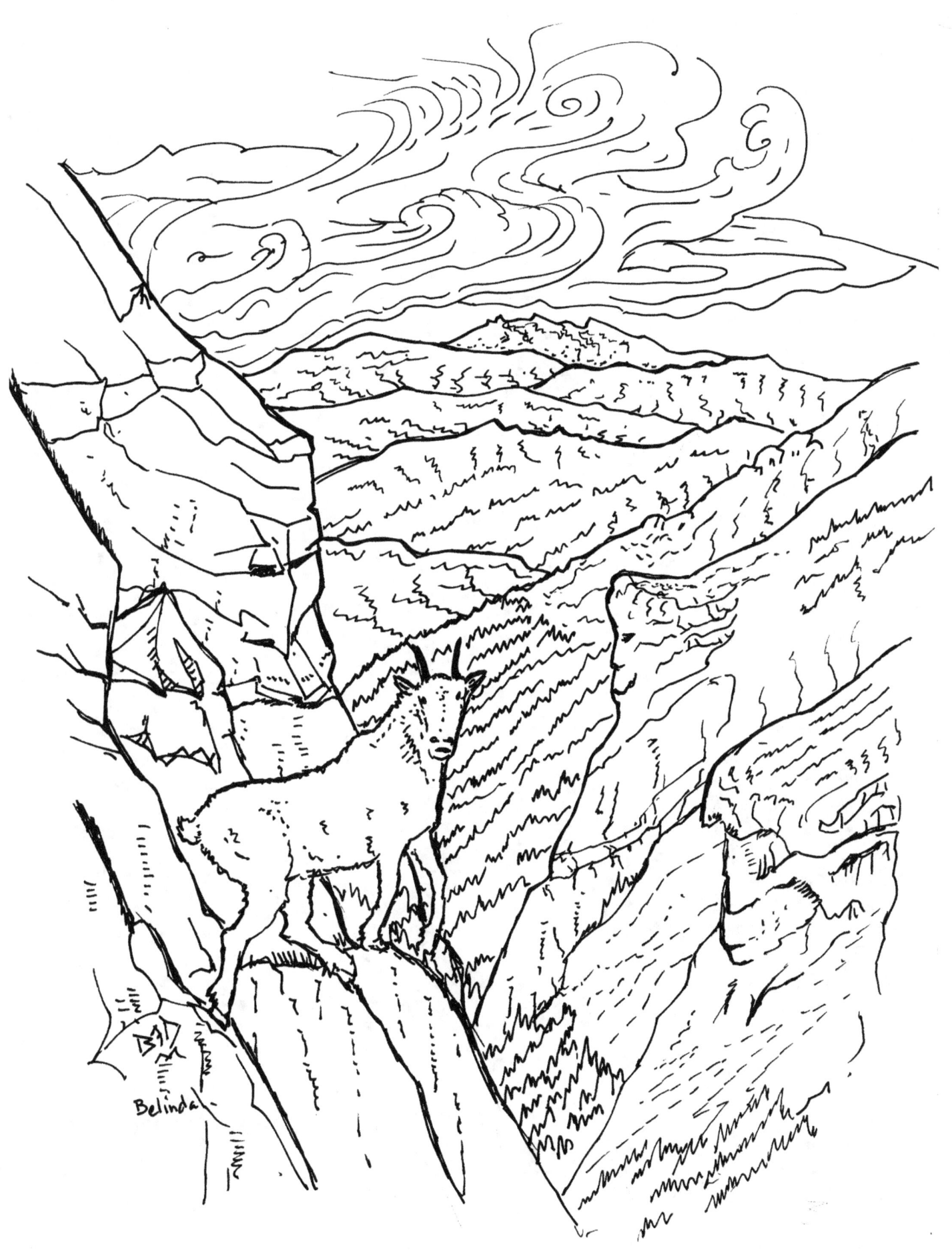

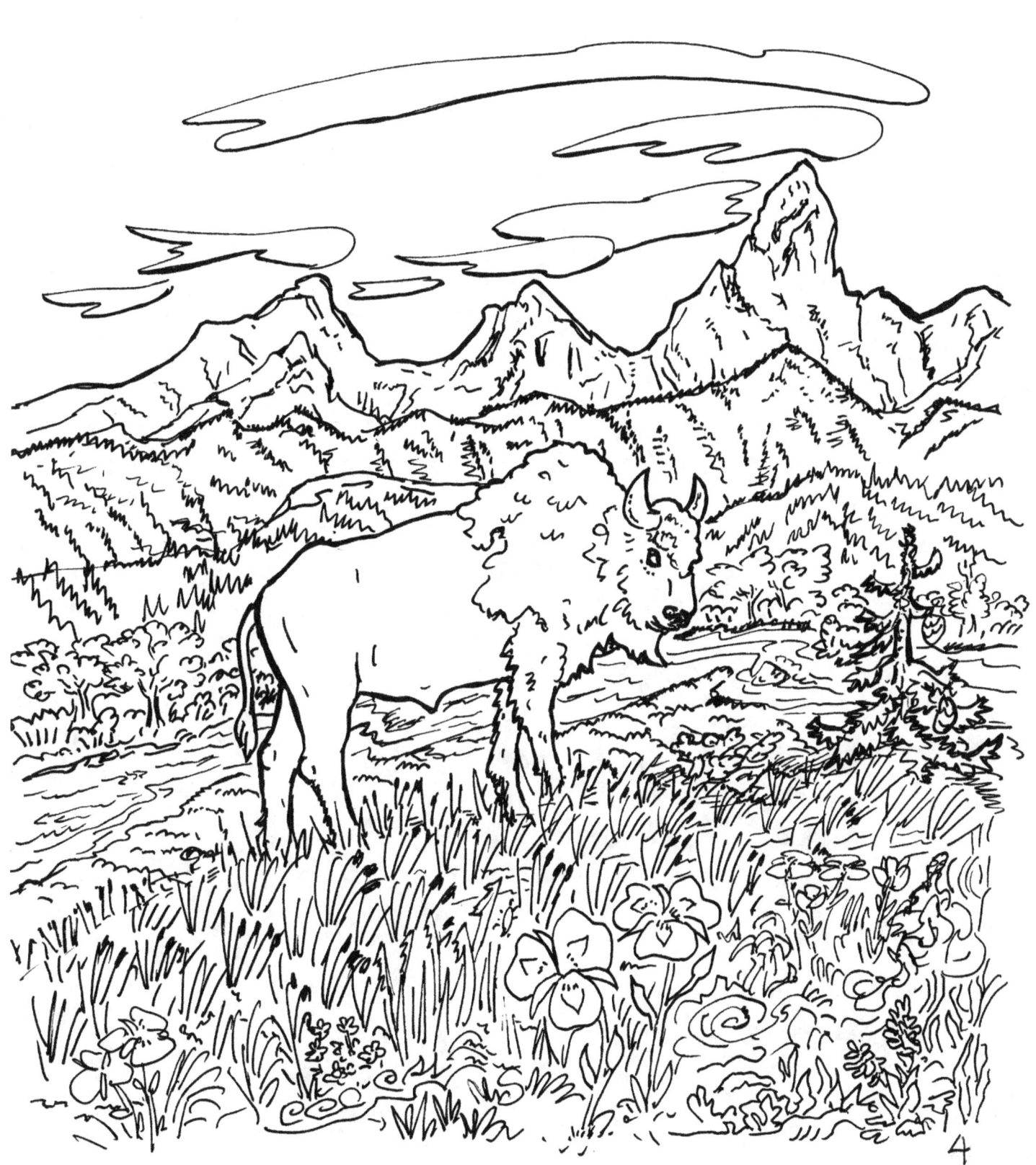

4

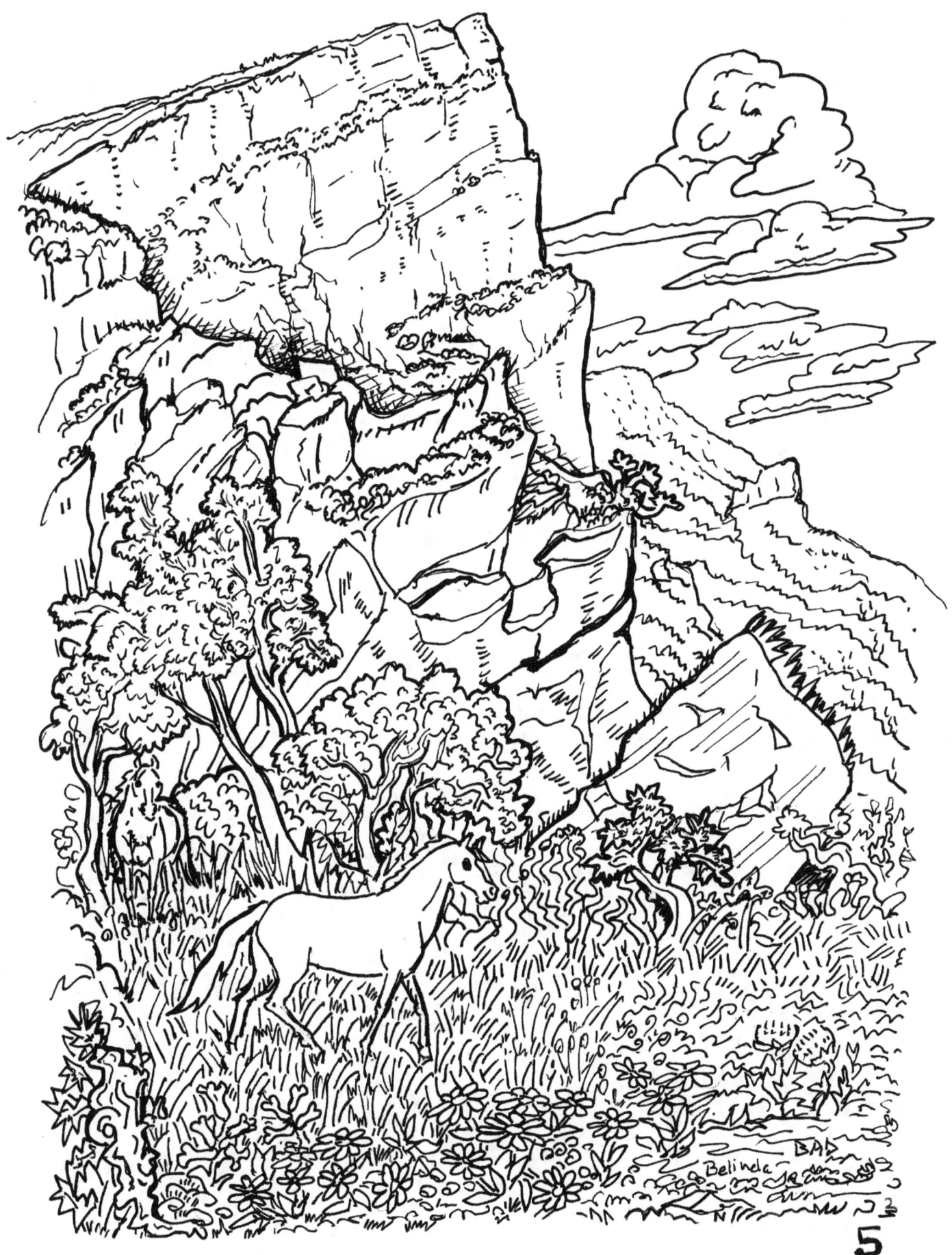

5

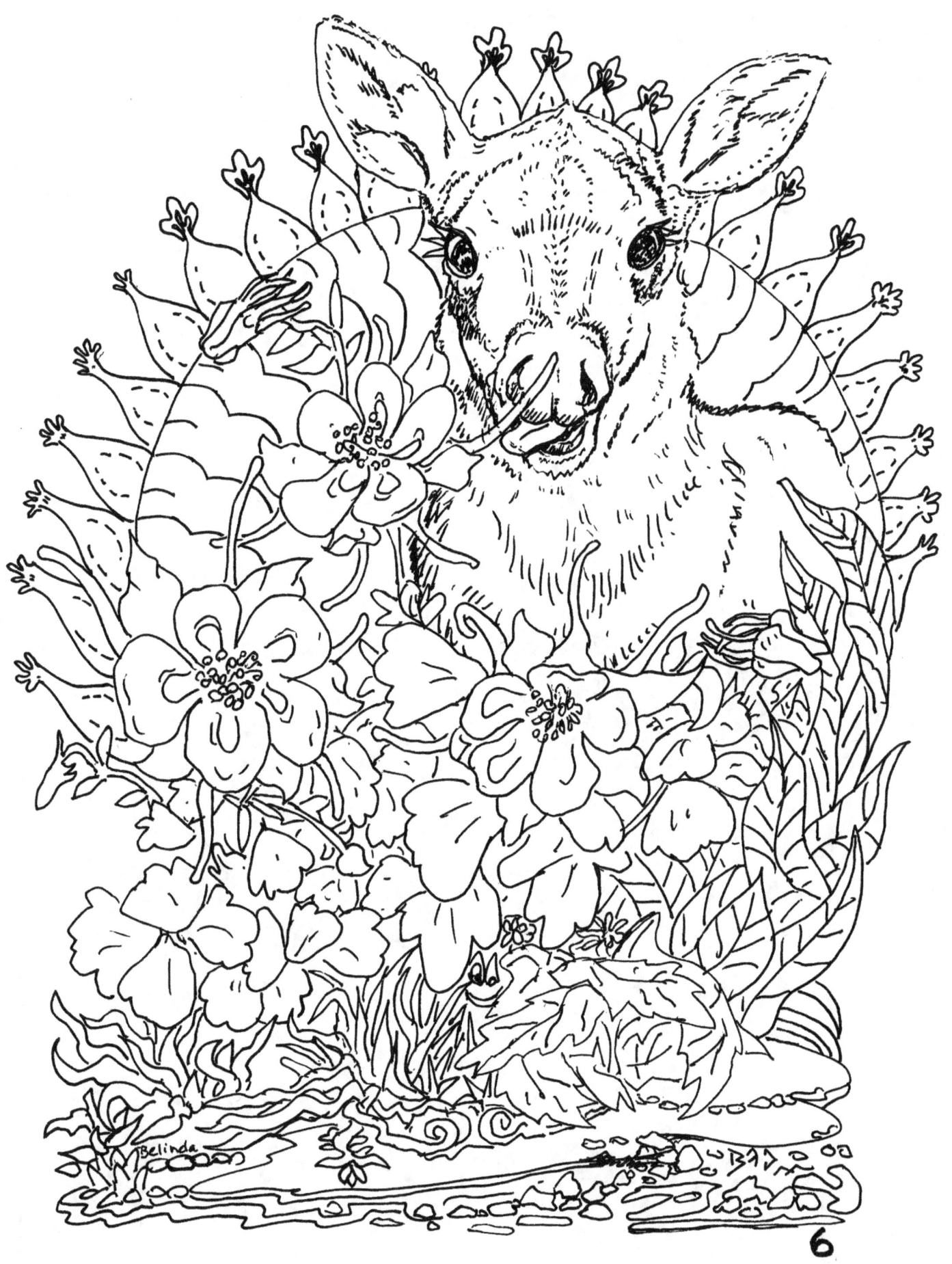

Belinda

6

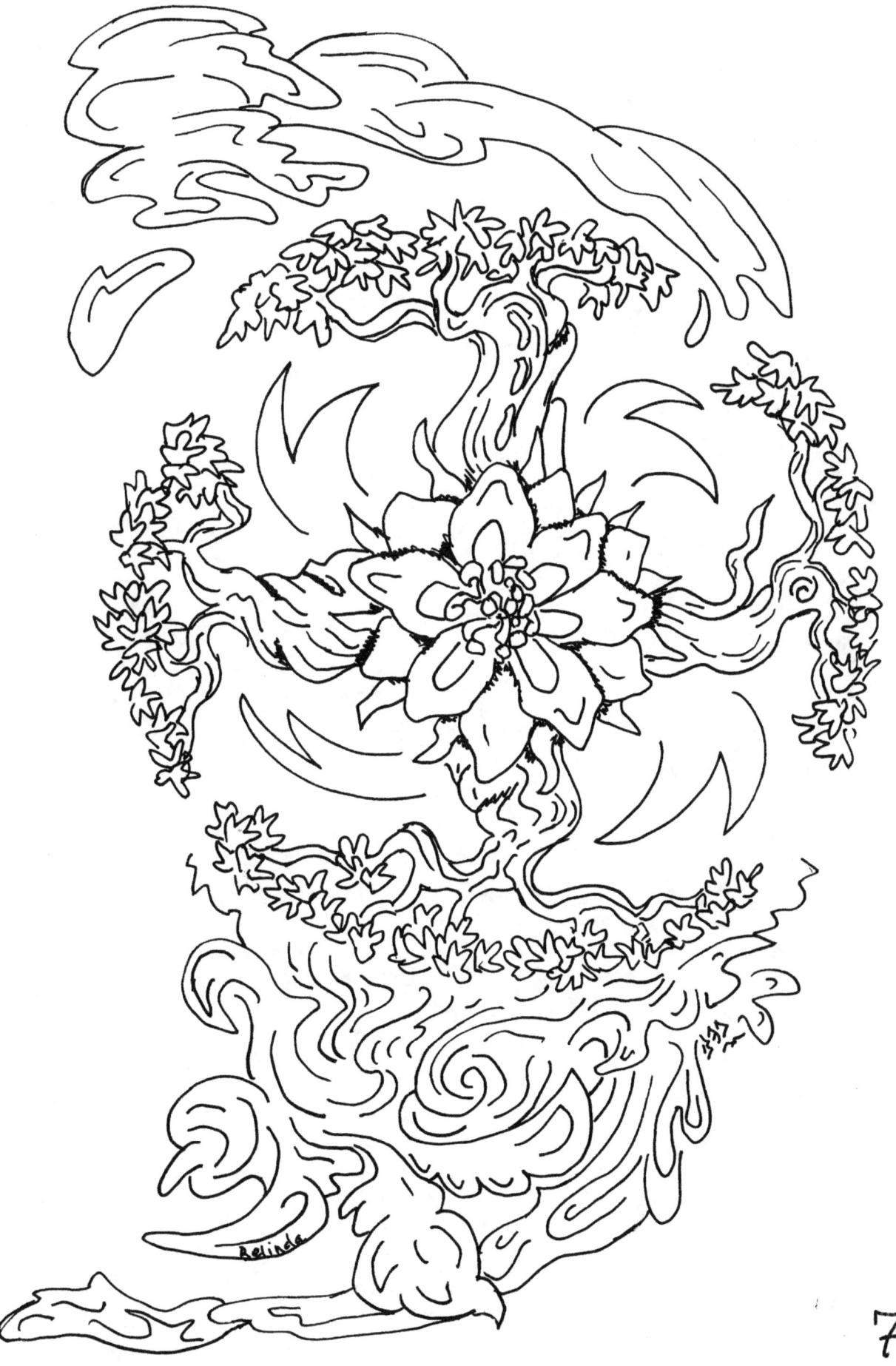

Belinda

7

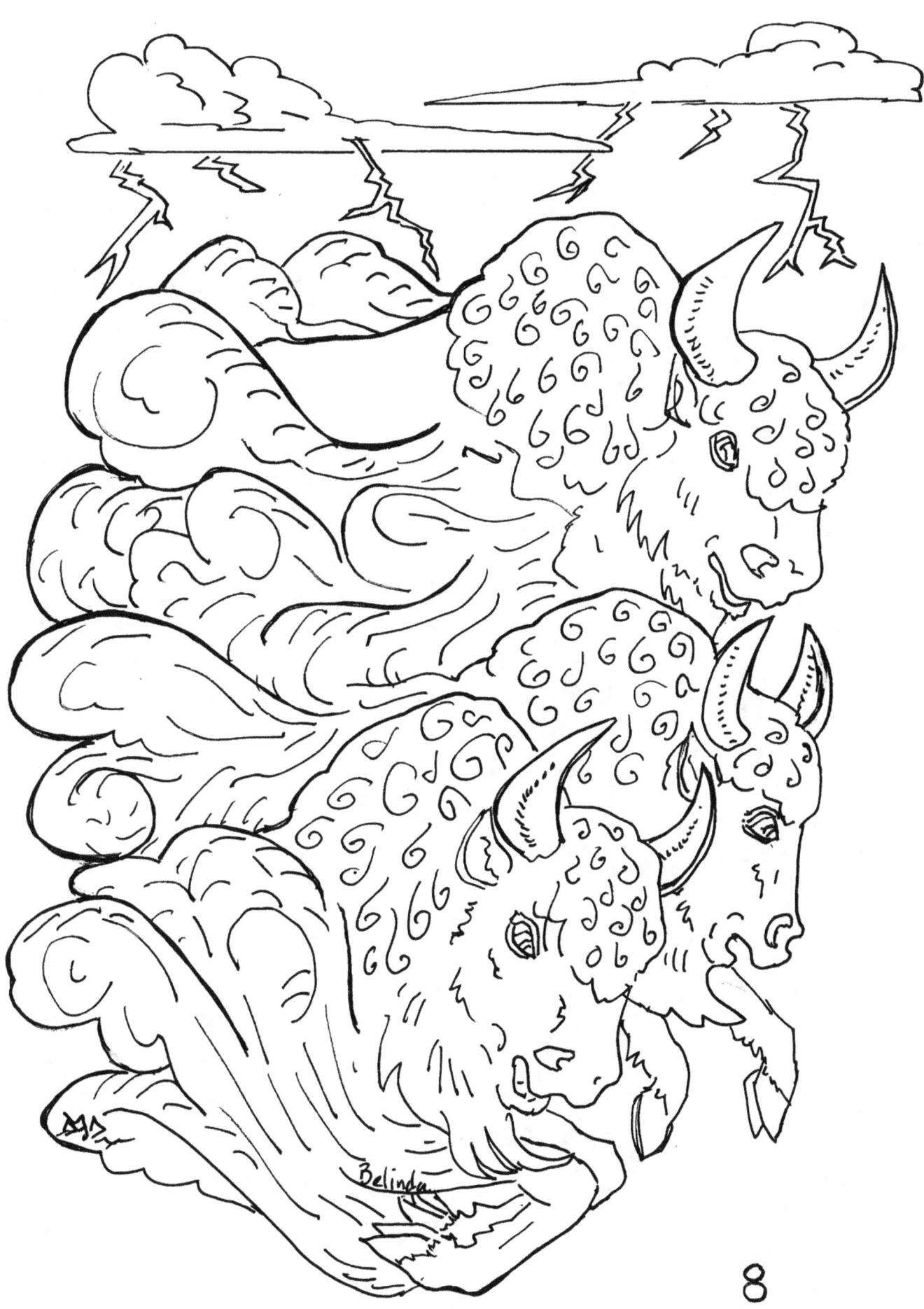

8

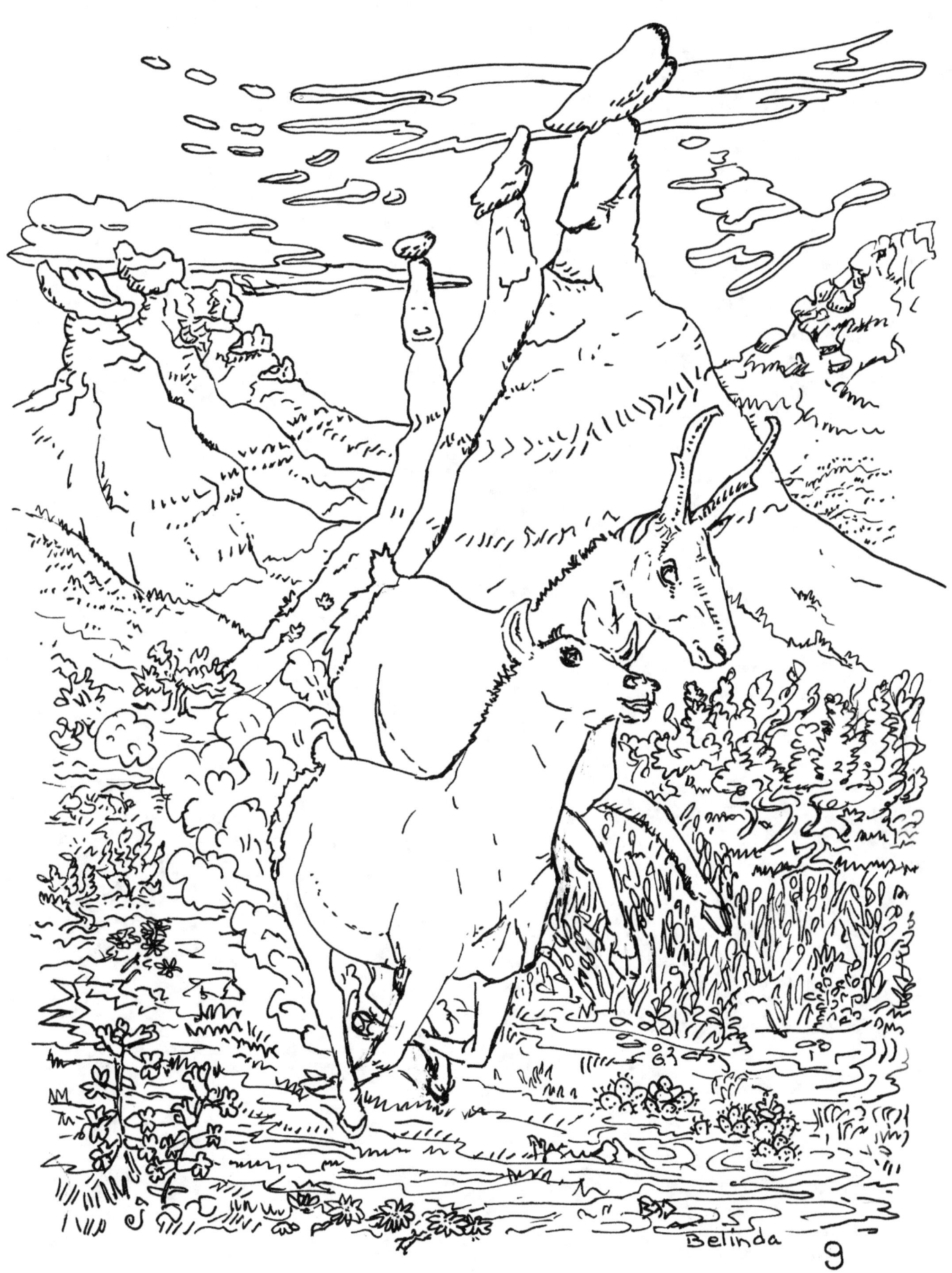

Belinda

9

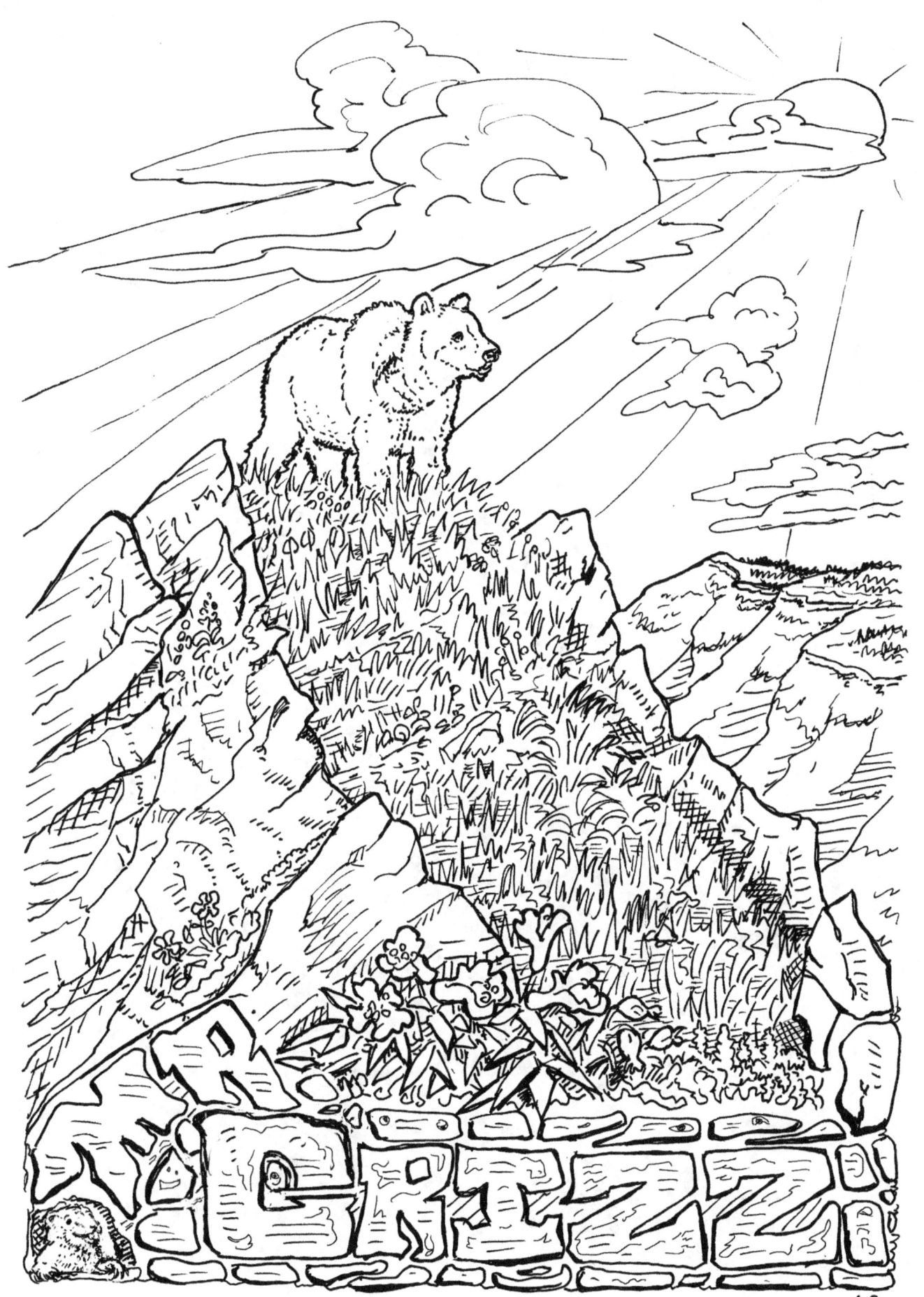

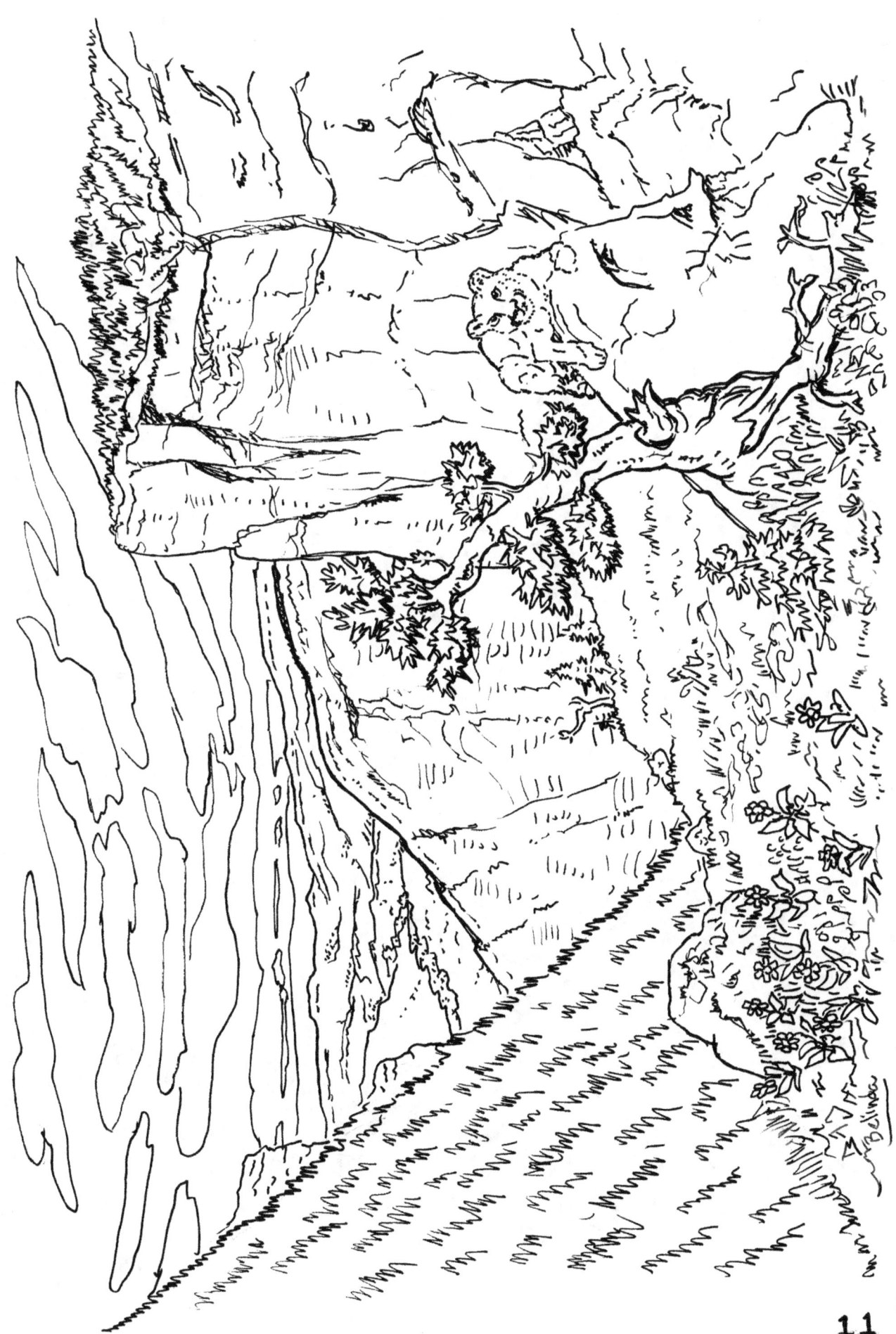

11

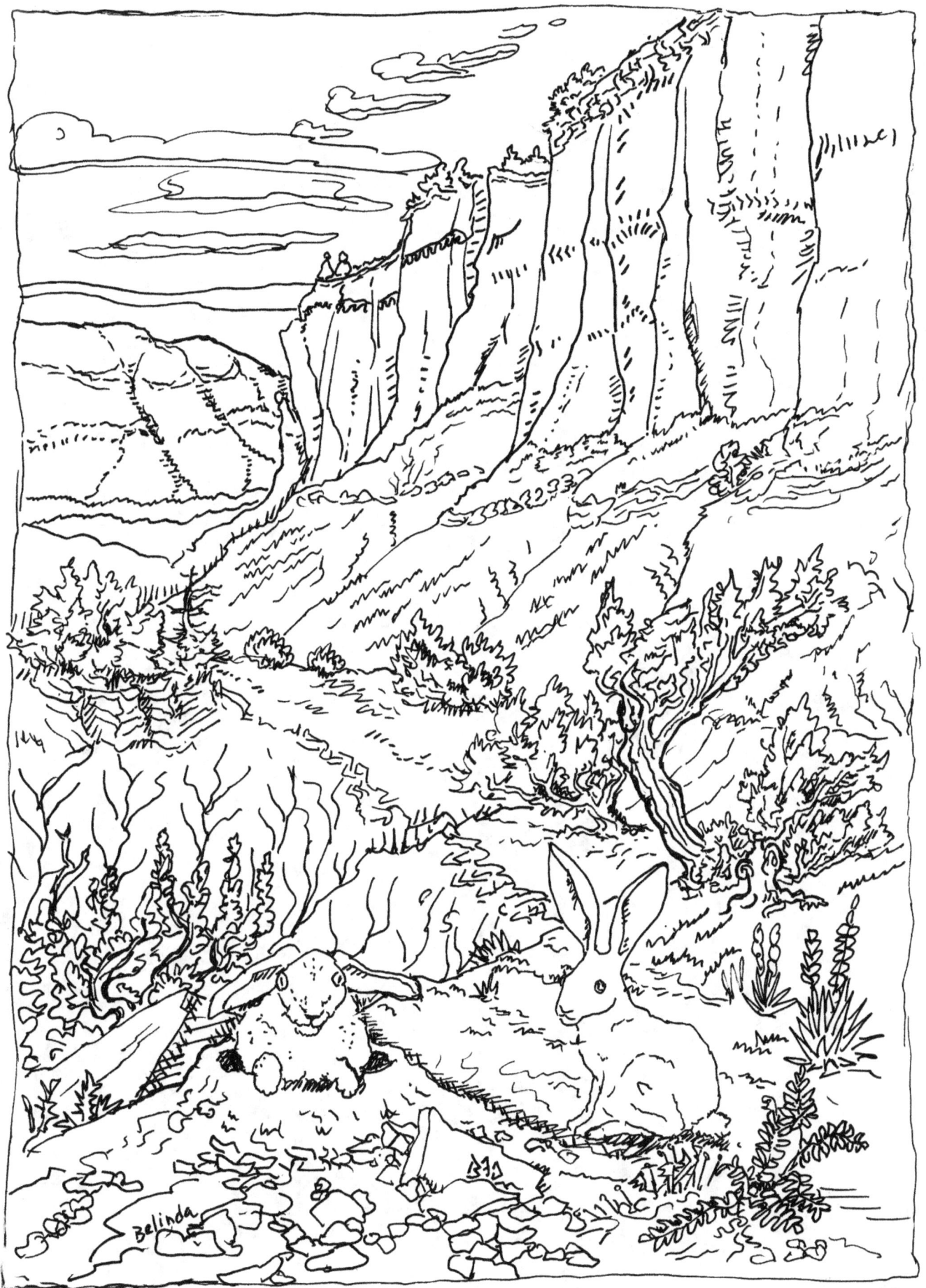

Belinda

12

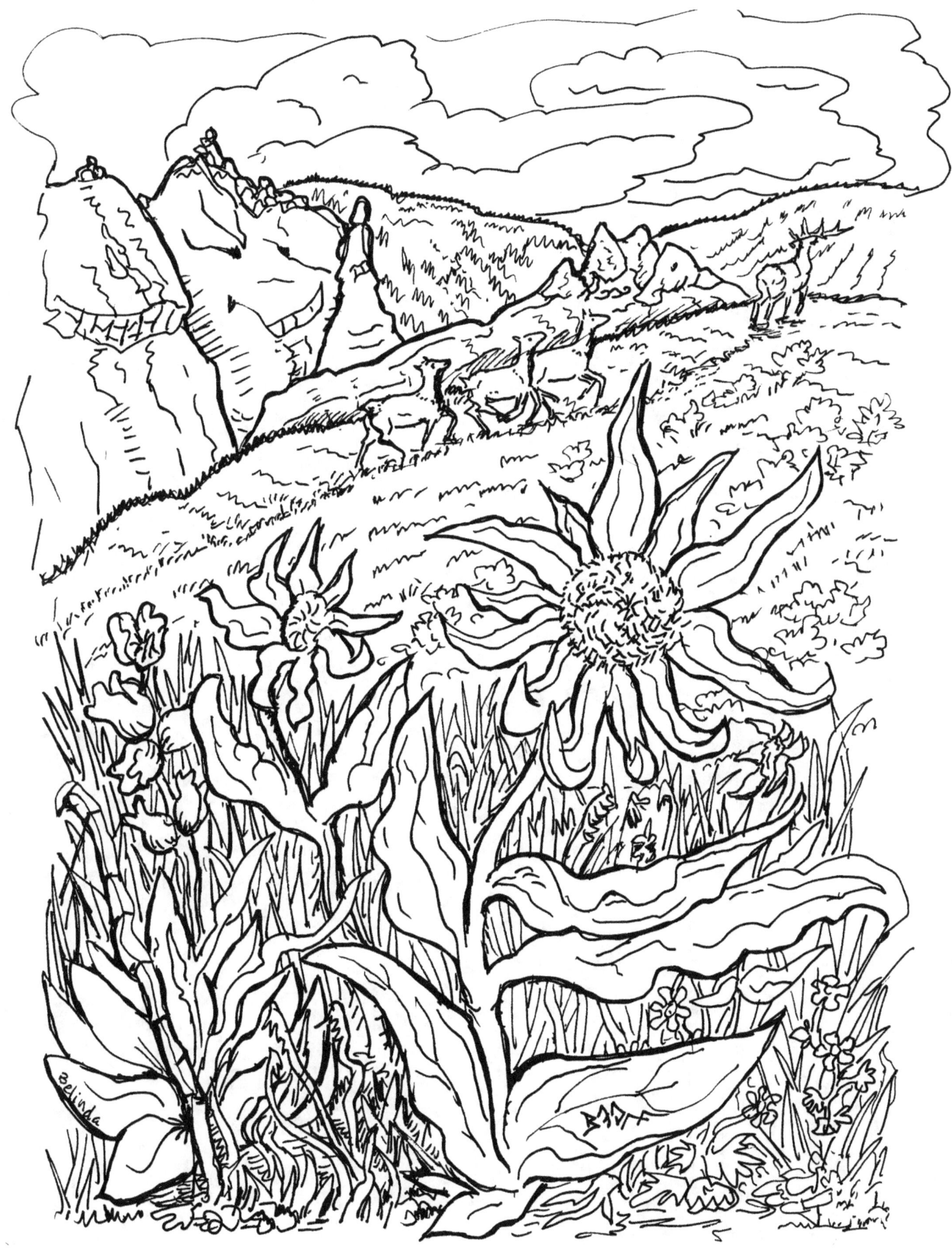

13

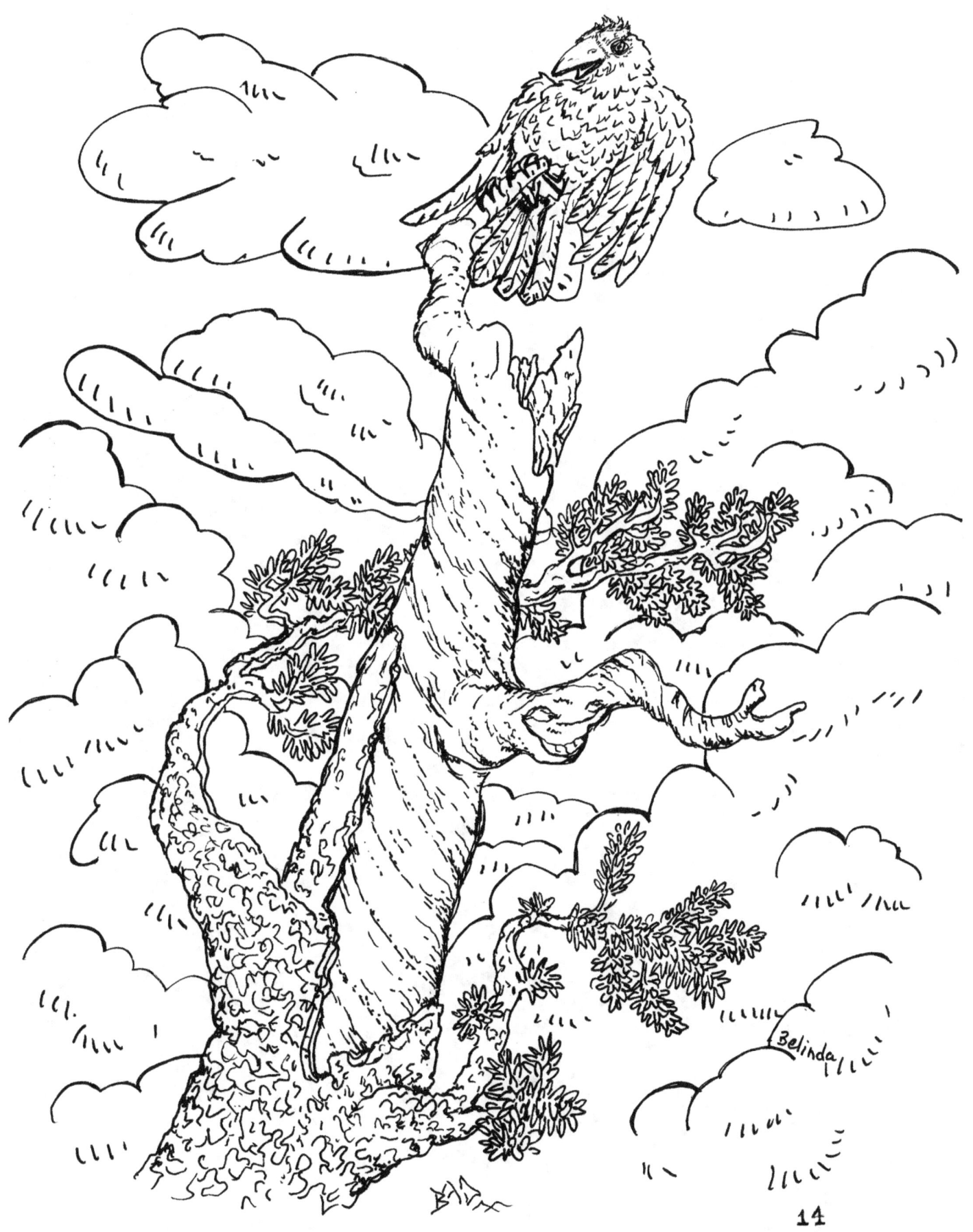

14

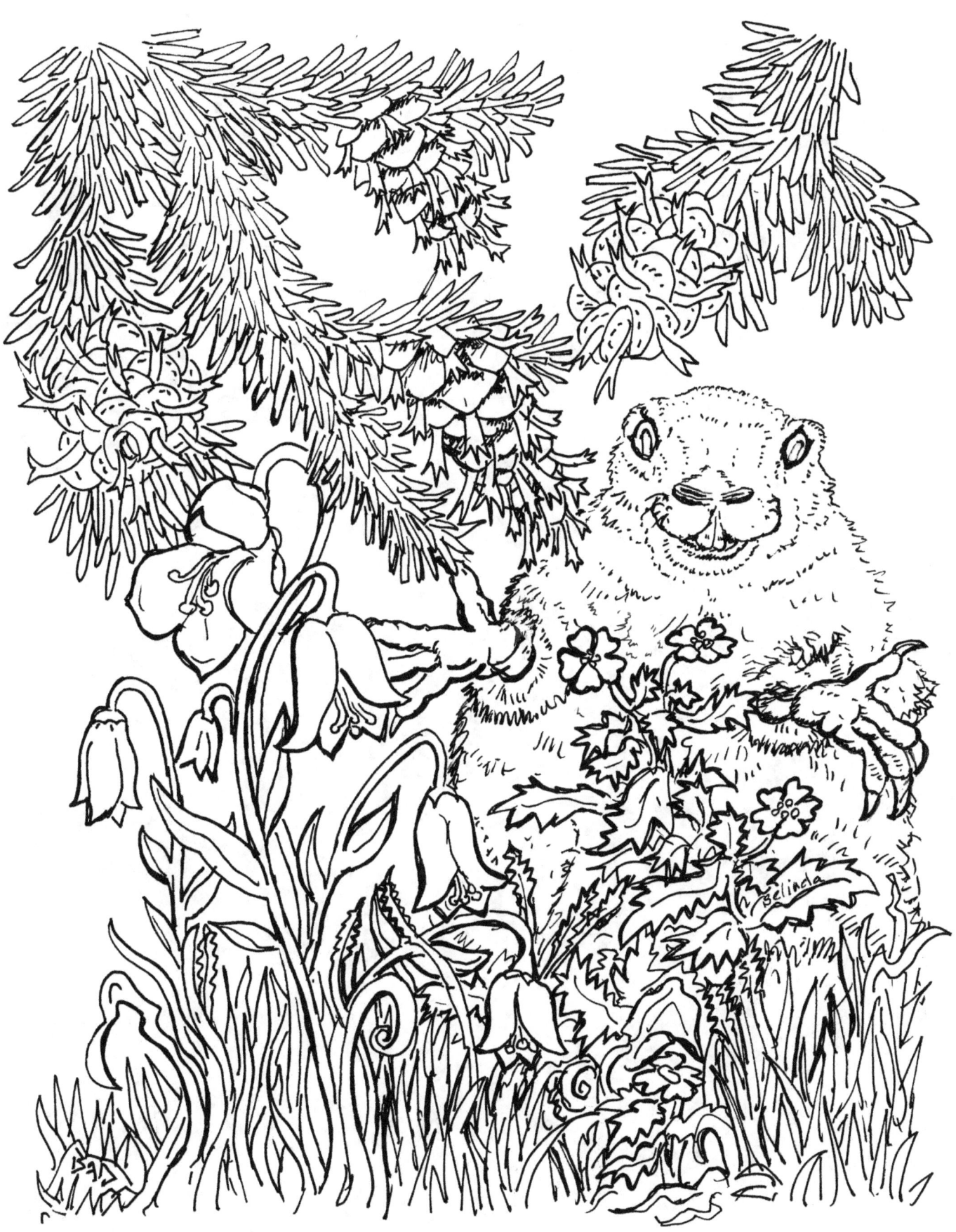

15

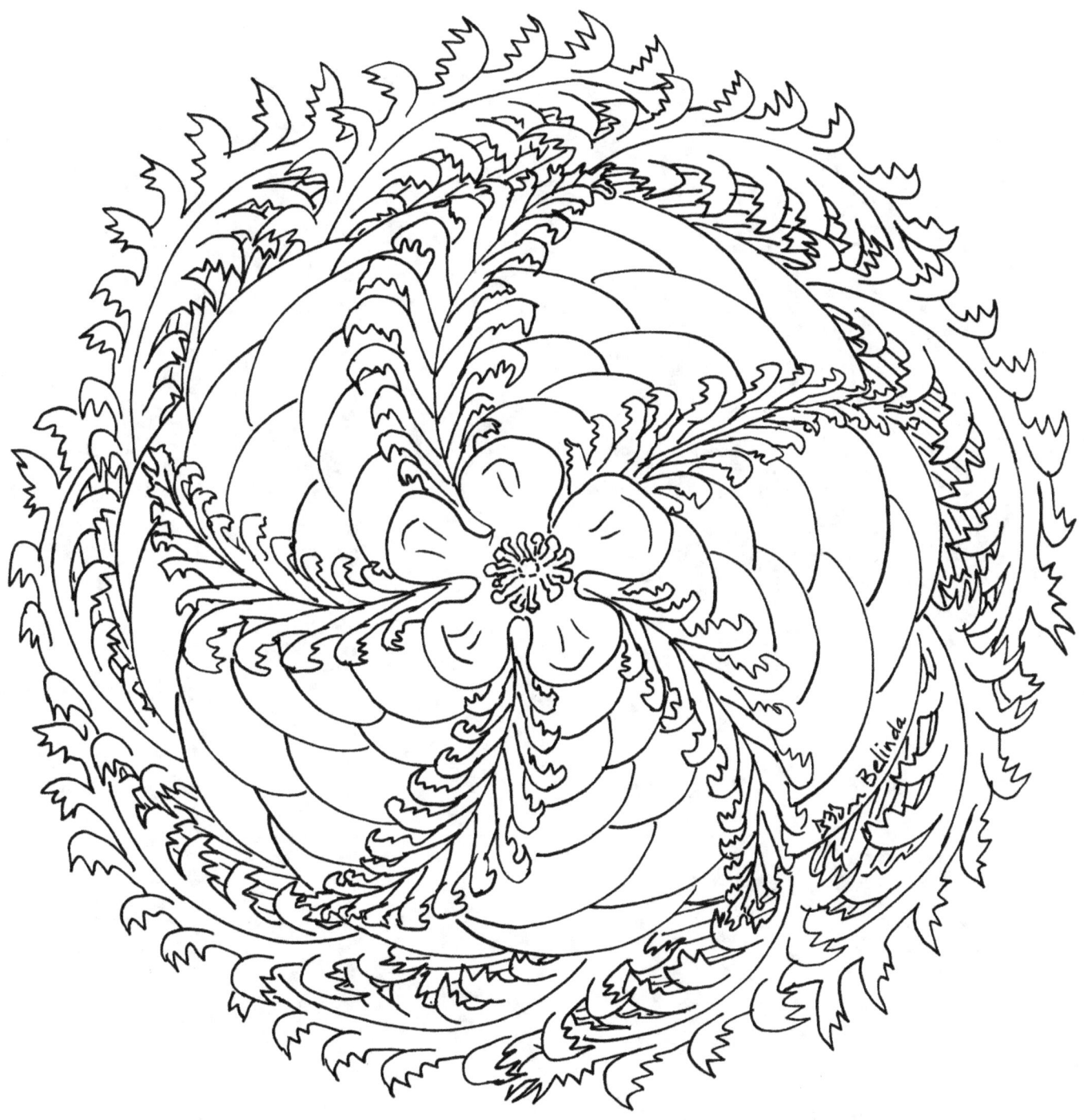

16

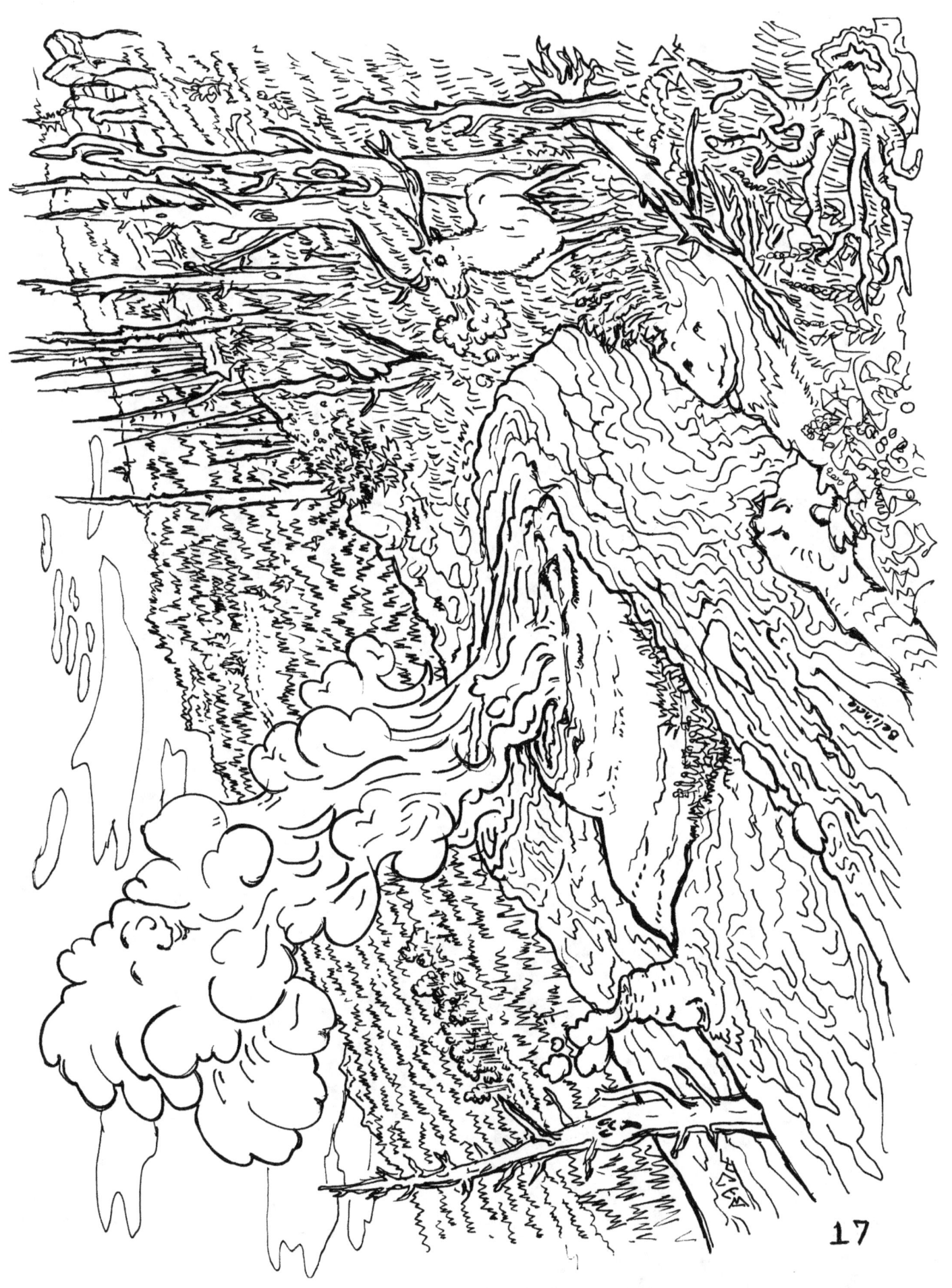

17

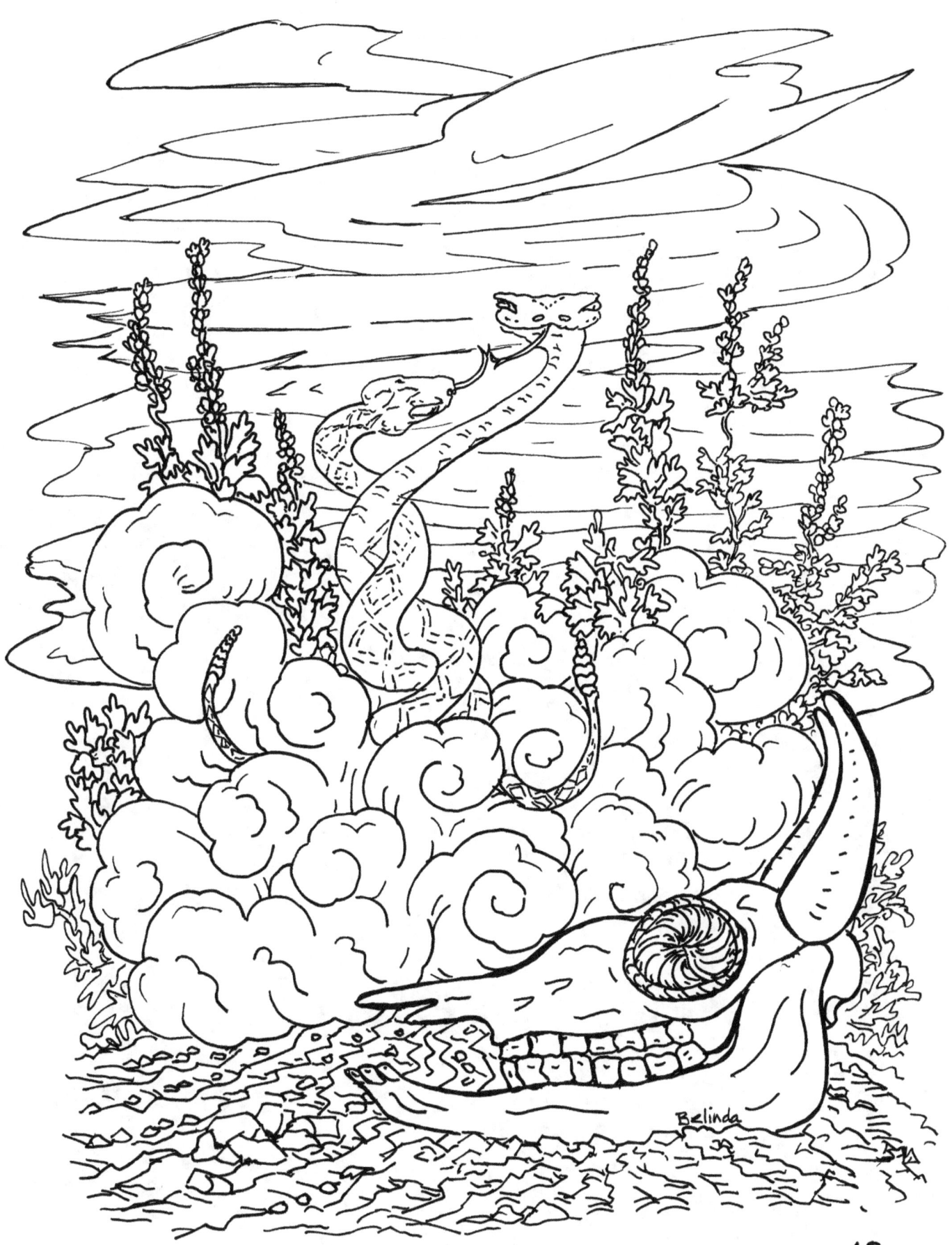

18

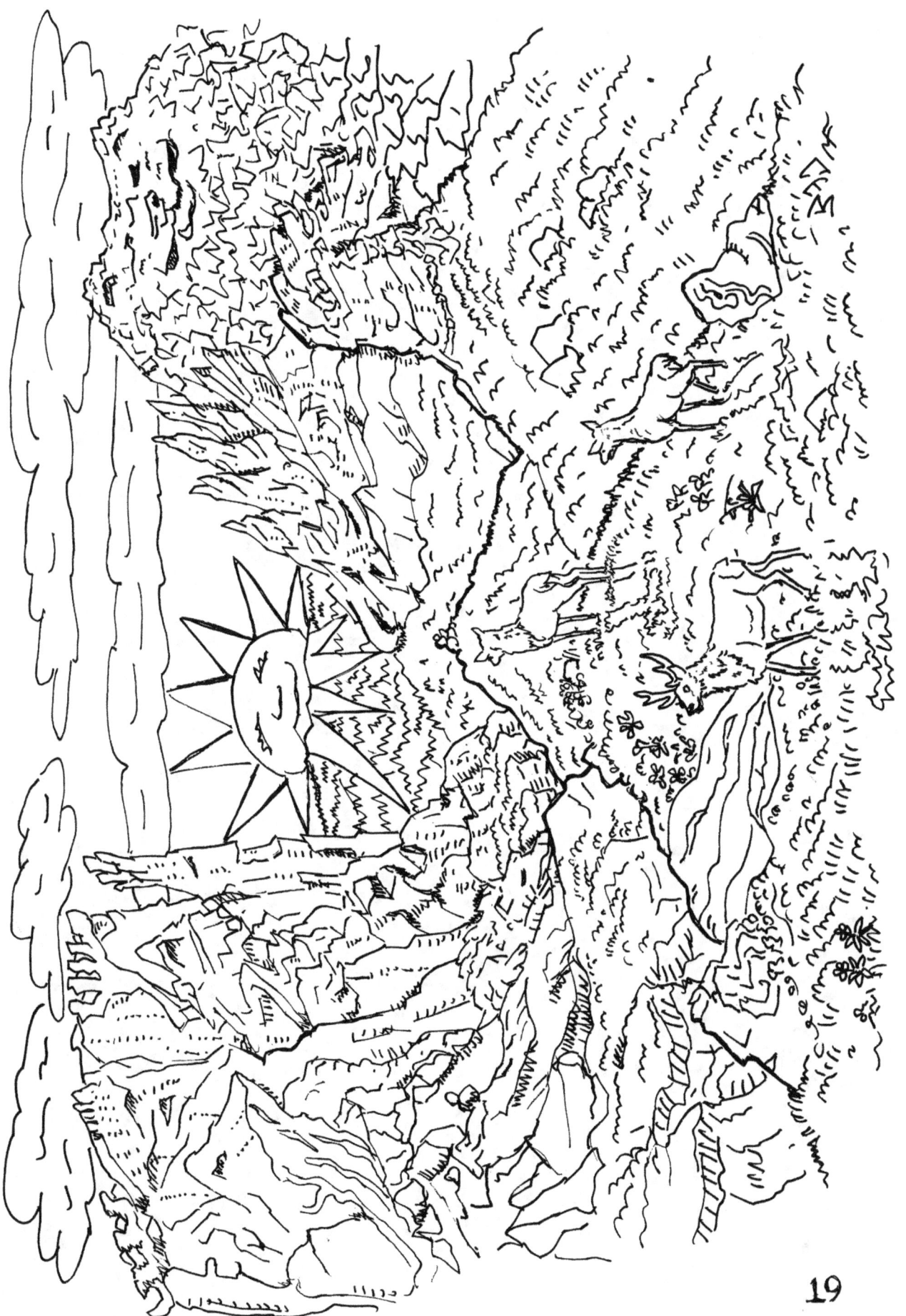

19

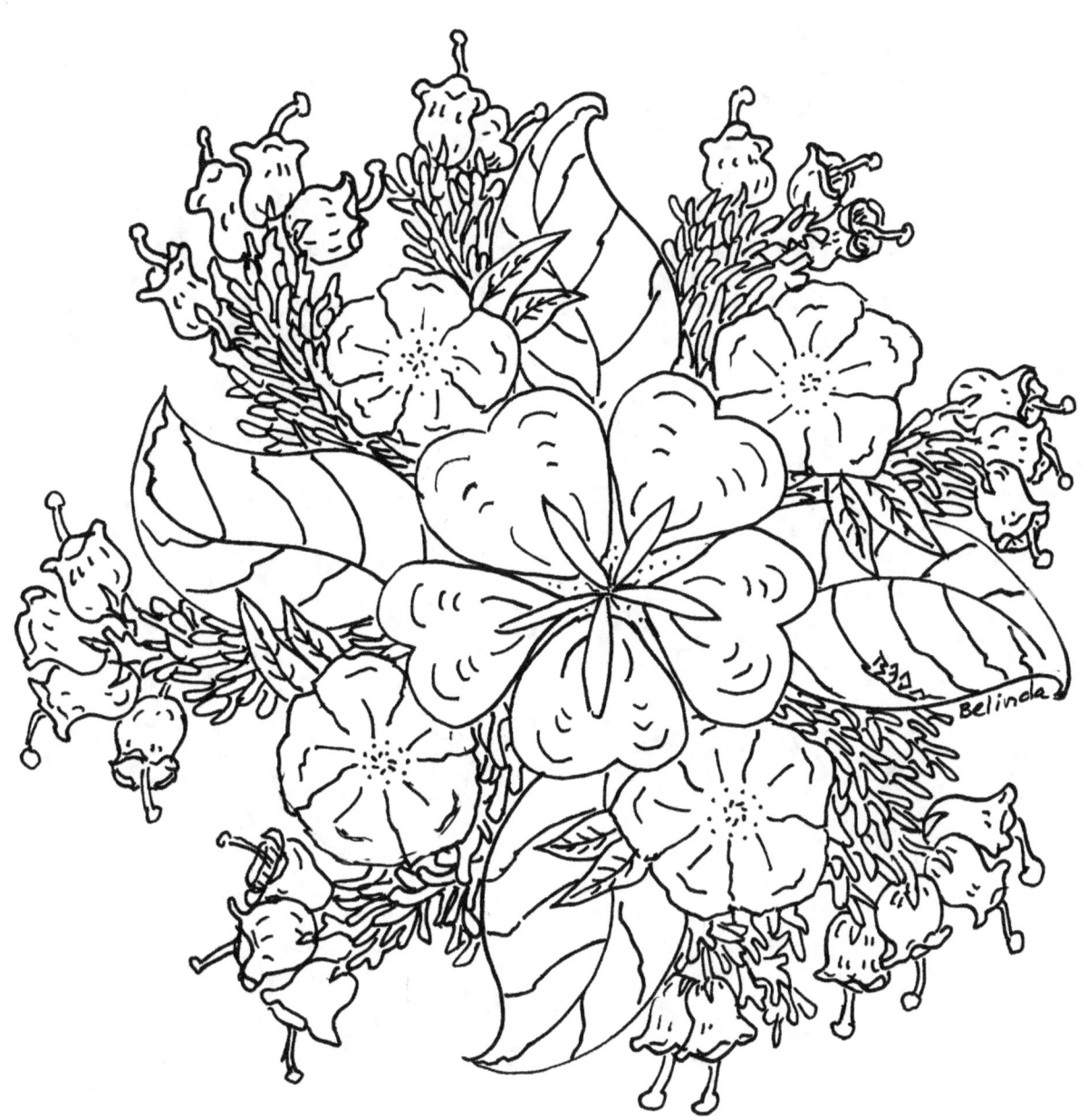

20

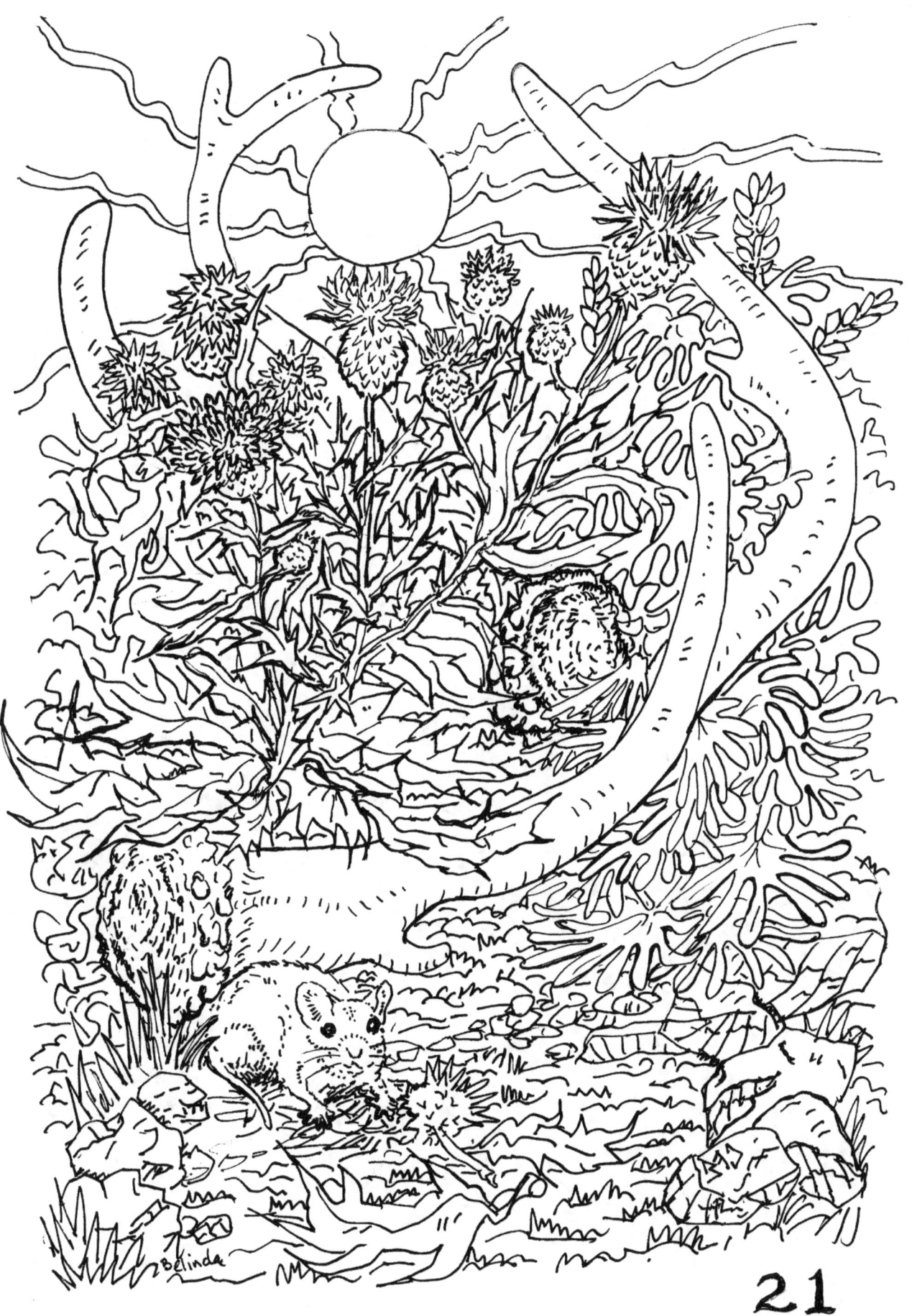

21

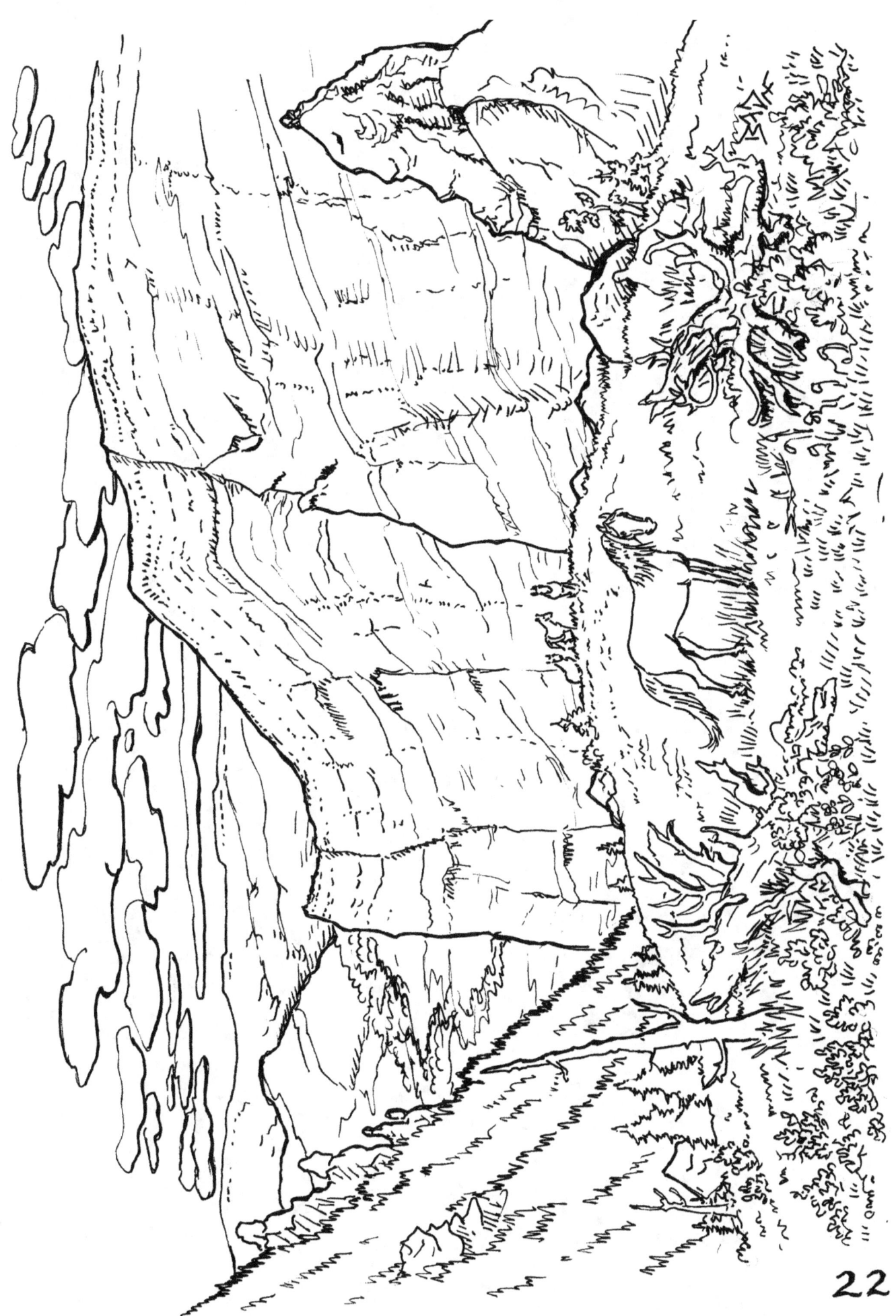

22

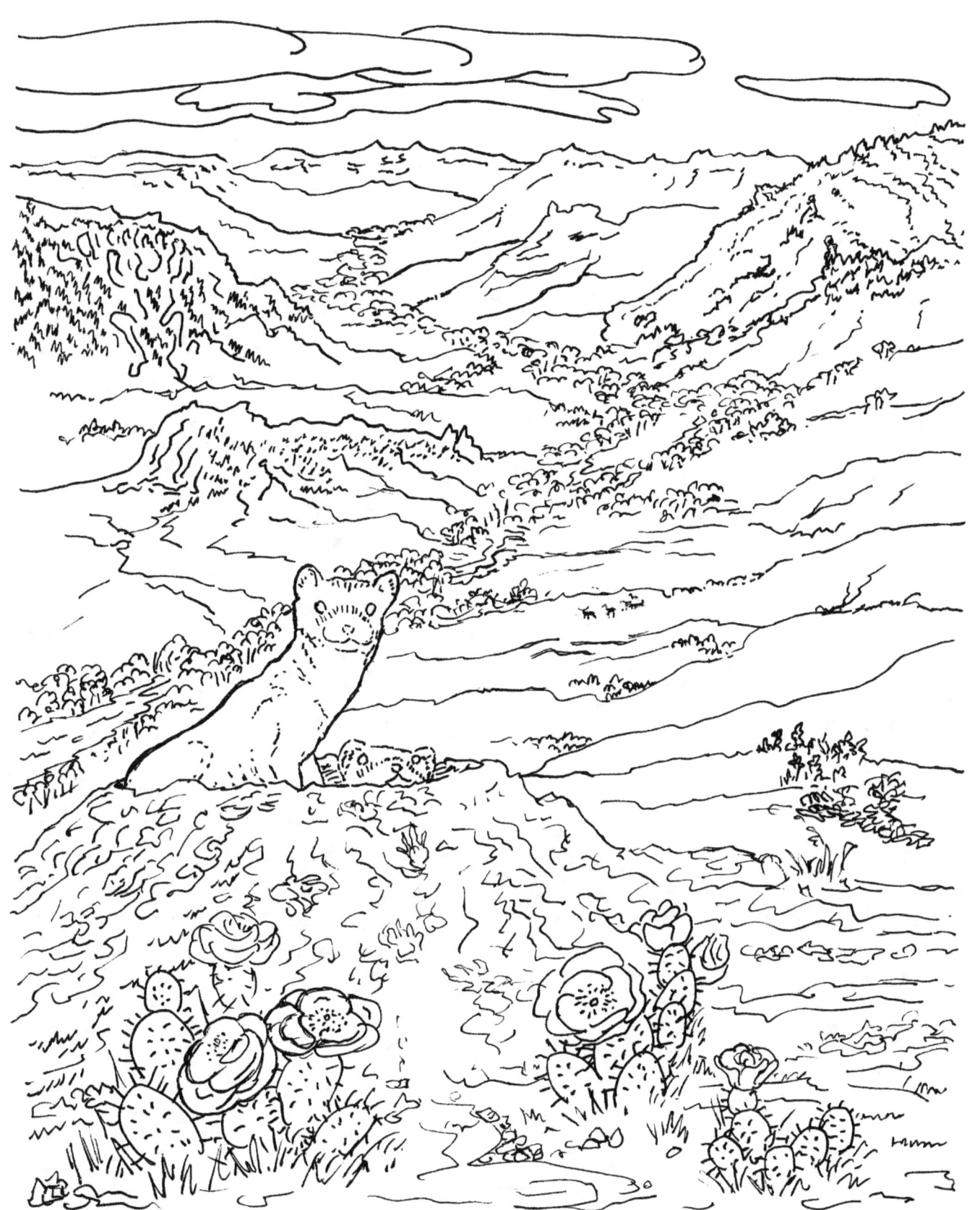

23

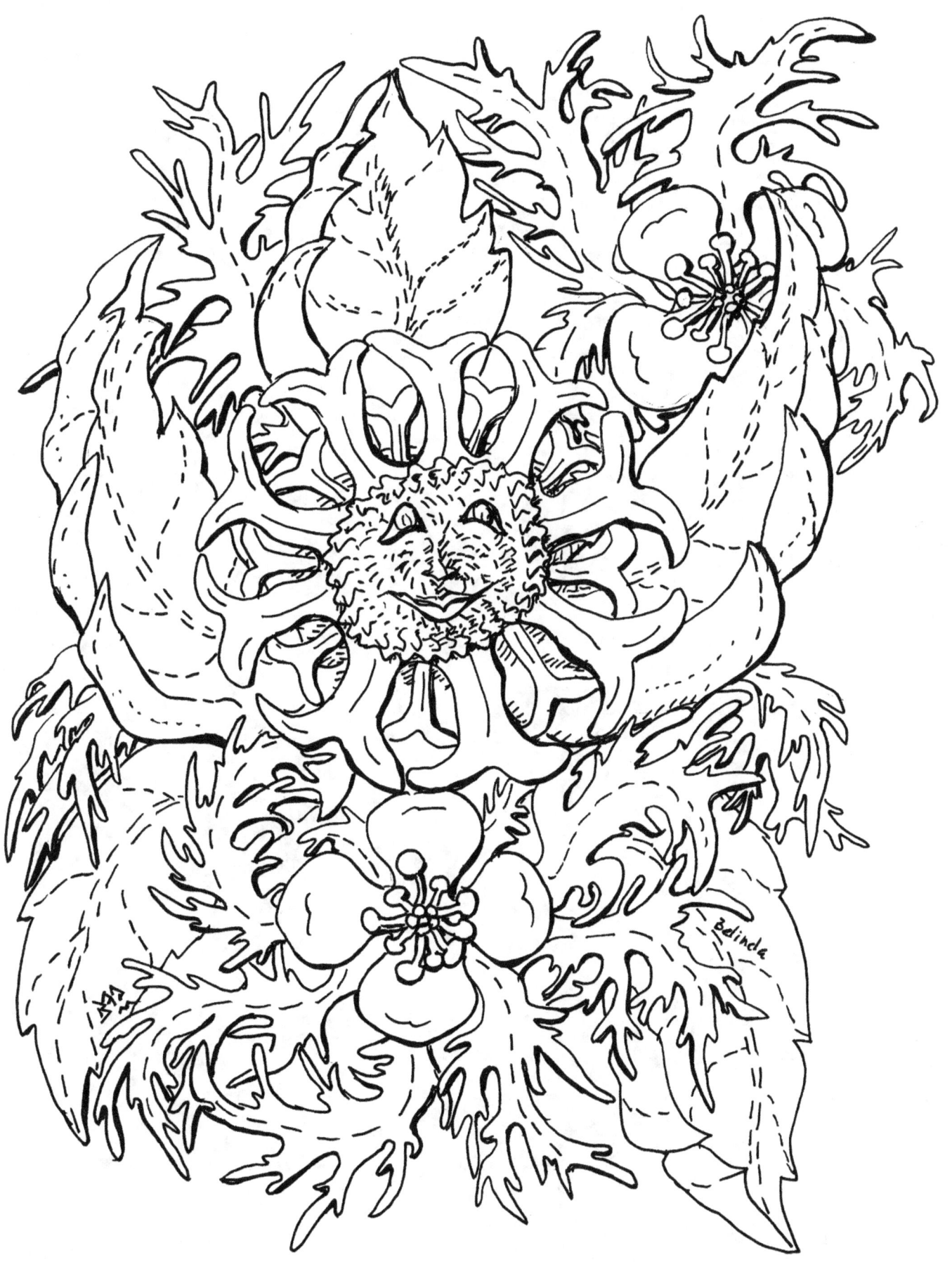

24

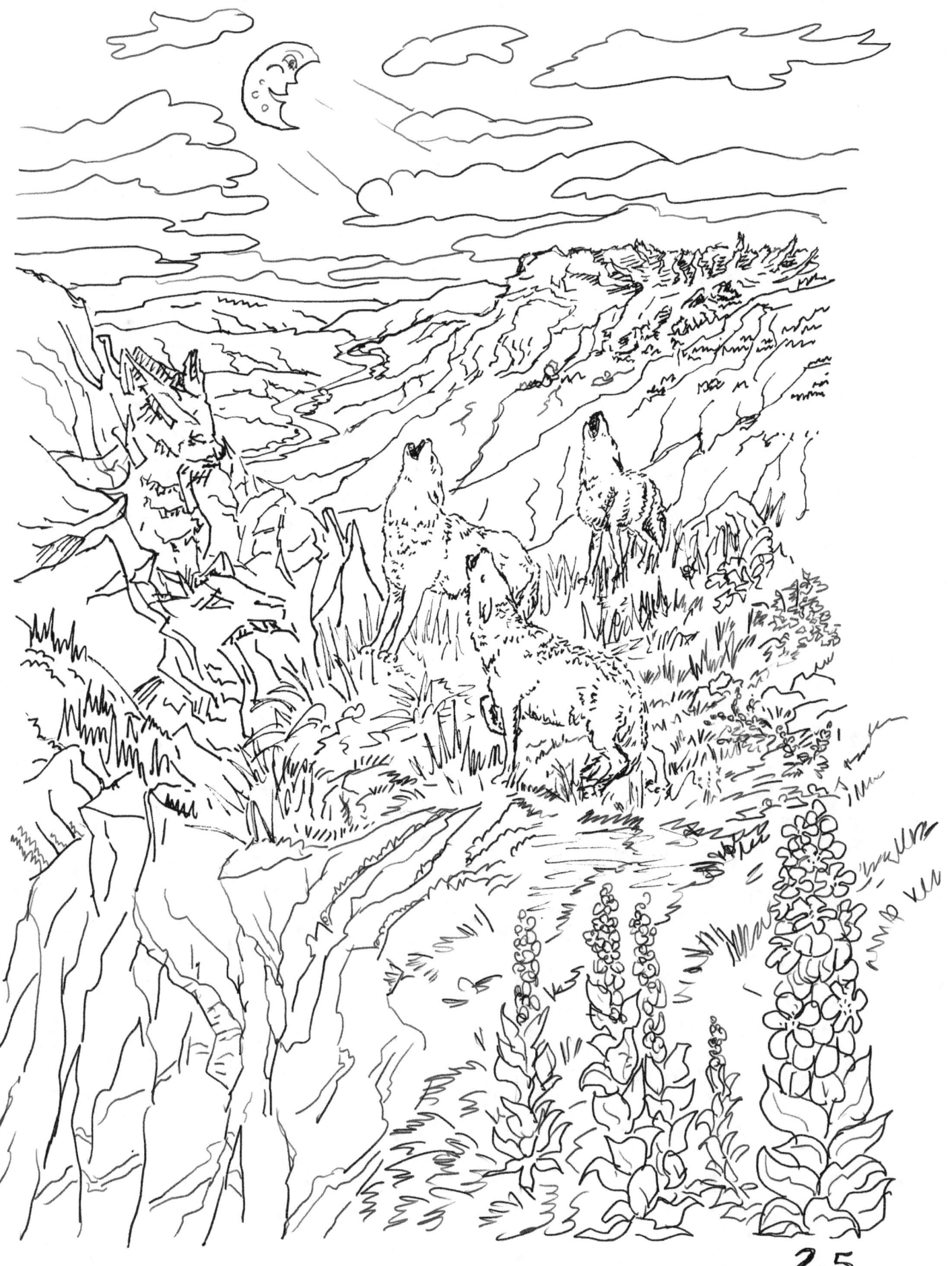

25